Speaking and Listening Learning Stations Grades 6–8

English Language Arts Series

Authors:	Schyrlet Cameron and Suzanne Myers
Editor:	Mary Dieterich
Proofreader:	Cindy Neisen and Margaret Brown

COPYRIGHT © 2017 Mark Twain Media, Inc.

ISBN 978-1-62223-637-4

Printing No. CD-404258

Mark Twain Media, Inc., Publishers
Distributed by Carson-Dellosa Publishing LLC

Visit us at www.carsondellosa.com

Table of Contents

To the Teacher

The Common Core State Standards address standards for English Language Arts, which includes standards for Speaking and Listening. The book *Speaking and Listening Learning Stations, Grades 6–8* is the latest addition to the Mark Twain Media *English Language Arts (ELA)* series.

In the *ELA* series, students in grades six through eight explore reading, writing, language, speaking, and listening skills in a learning-station environment. Learning stations engage students in individual or small-group activities and are an instructional strategy that can be used to target specific skills.

Each book in the *ELA* series features five or six units of study. Each unit has a teacher page that identifies the goal, states the standards, lists materials and setup for the activities, and provides instructions to be presented to students. Also, there are questions for opening discussion and student reflection. (Note: It is important for the teacher to introduce, model, or review the concepts or skills with the students at the beginning of each unit.)

Speaking and Listening Learning Stations, Grades 6–8 contains five units of study. Each unit addresses the Speaking and Listening section of the ELA Common Core State Standards. The units can be taught within the English Language Arts content area or can be used as interdisciplinary units between English Language Arts and other subject areas.

Each unit consists of four or five learning stations that address presentation literacy skills. The activity at each station is designed to create interest, provide practice, and stimulate discussion. Some activities have accompanying handouts. Whenever applicable, the use of technology is integrated into an activity. The Research unit is designed to be used with students' current interactive notebooks, or they can make mini notebooks for this unit.

Other Books in the ELA Series

- ***Reading: Literature Learning Stations, Grades 6–8***
  The units focus on alliteration, rhyme, plot and setting, tone and mood, and poetry.

- ***Reading: Informational Text Learning Stations, Grades 6–8***
  The units focus on citing evidence, bias, point of view, propaganda techniques, organizational text structures, and text features.

- ***Writing Learning Stations, Grades 6–8***
  The units focus on fact and opinion, characterization, making inferences, proofreading, and dialogue.

- ***Language Learning Stations, Grades 6–8***
  The units focus on punctuation, dictionary usage, figurative language, roots and affixes, and word meaning.

- ***Literacy in History and Social Studies Learning Station Activities to Meet CCSS, Grades 6–8***
  The units focus on analyzing text, making inferences, and citing textual evidence, using primary and secondary sources.

- ***Literacy in Science and Technology Learning Station Activities to Meet CCSS, Grades 6–8***
  The units focus on following multi-step procedures, analyzing textual and visual information, and summarizing textual information.

Common Core State Standards Matrix

English Language Arts Standards: Speaking and Listening

Units of Study	SL.6.1	SL.6.2	SL.6.3	SL.6.4	SL.6.5	SL.6.6	SL.7.1	SL.7.2	SL.7.3	SL.7.4	SL.7.5	SL.7.6	SL.8.1	SL.8.2	SL.8.3	SL.8.4	SL.8.5	SL.8.6
Research (Interactive Notebook)	X						X						X					
Opinions, Claims, and Evidence			X	X					X	X					X	X		
Multimedia Components and Visual Displays		X			X			X			X			X			X	
Verbal and Nonverbal Communication				X						X						X		
Collegial Discussions	X						X						X					

Teacher Page

Unit: Research (Interactive Notebook)

Goal: Students will demonstrate skills needed to conduct research.

Common Core State Standards (CCSS):

6th Grade	7th Grade	8th Grade
SL.6.1.A Come to discussions prepared, having read or studied required material; explicitly draw on that preparation by referring to evidence on the topic, text, or issue to probe and reflect on ideas under discussion.	SL.7.1.A Come to discussions prepared, having read or researched material under study; explicitly draw on that preparation by referring to evidence on the topic, text, or issue to probe and reflect on ideas under discussion.	SL.8.1.A Come to discussions prepared, having read or researched material under study; explicitly draw on that preparation by referring to evidence on the topic, text, or issue to probe and reflect on ideas under discussion

© Copyright 2010. National Governors Association Center for Best Practices and Council of Chief State School Officers. All rights reserved.

Materials List/Setup

Station One: *Locating Sources*
    Student Instructions
    Right-hand Interactive Notebook Page
    Learning Station Activity

Station Two: *Keyword Search*
    Student Instructions
    Right-hand Interactive Notebook Page
    Learning Station Activity

Station Three: *Evaluating Internet Sources*
    Student Instructions
    Right-hand Interactive Notebook Page
    Learning Station Activity
    Handout: *Battle of Gettysburg Websites*

Station Four: *Creating a Bibliography*
    Student Instructions
    Right-hand Interactive Notebook Page
    Learning Station Activity
    Handout: *How to Format a Bilbiography*
    4 sources*

*Will need four sources: book, encyclopedia article, magazine article, and webpage
One copy of Student Instructions, Right-hand Interactive Notebook, Learning Station Activity, and Handout pages per student
If students are not already using interactive notebooks, they can use the pages to create mini notebooks for this unit.

Opening: Discussion Questions (Teacher-Directed)

1. What are the steps in the research process?
2. Where can you locate resources?
3. How do you know if a source is credible and reliable?
4. What is the best way to keep track of your sources?

Student Instructions for Learning Stations

At each learning station, you will read the student instruction page. Use the information to create your right-hand interactive notebook page. Apply the information to help you with the learning station activity.

Closure: Reflection

Think about what you learned from the "Research (Interactive Notebook)" unit. Be prepared to share your thoughts during one-on-one, small-group, or classroom discussion.

Student Instructions—Station One: *Locating Sources*

Introduction

Read the following information. Use what you learn to complete the right-hand interactive notebook page.

You've chosen your topic, and you are now ready to start the research process. Where do you begin? An excellent place to start is your school library. The school library provides a wide variety of resources. Information can be located in print or online sources. School libraries also provide access to the Internet. Be sure to ask the librarian for help on locating or accessing resources. Don't forget to check out the public library for additional resources.

Common Types of Sources

Books provide in-depth coverage on topics, but the information may not be current. Use the online card catalog to search the library's book collection. Most online card catalogs can be searched by author, title, subject, and keyword.

Encyclopedias are available in print or online. Two types of encyclopedias are general and subject. General encyclopedias cover a wide variety of topics, while a subject encyclopedia covers a specific subject area. Encyclopedias are useful for gaining background information on a topic; however, the articles only provide a limited overview, and the information may not be up to date.

A **periodical database** is a collection of newspaper, magazine, and journal articles. Articles focus on recent developments or specific issues about a topic but do not provide broad coverage.

The **Internet** can provide immediate access to information; however, it is important to make sure the information is reliable, credible, and up to date. Be sure to evaluate a website before using the information.

How to Create Your Right-hand Interactive Notebook Page

Complete the following steps on a blank page on the right-hand side of a notebook. If you already have an interactive notebook, complete these steps on a blank page on the right-hand side of your current interactive notebook.

Step 1: Cut out the title and glue it to the top of the notebook page.
Step 2: Cut around the outside border of the shutter fold. Create four flaps by cutting on the dark solid lines. Fold in half on the dotted line and glue the back of the shutter fold to the notebook page.
Step 3: Cut out the four word pieces. Glue a word piece to each of the outside flaps.
Step 4: Under each flap, write an advantage and a disadvantage of using information from that type of source.

Demonstrate and Reflect on What You Have Learned

Use the school library resources to complete the learning station activity. After completing the activity, write a reflection in your interactive notebook about your experience using the library resources.

Locating Sources

	Advantage: **Disadvantage:**
	Advantage: **Disadvantage:**
	Advantage: **Disadvantage:**
	Advantage: **Disadvantage:**

BOOK	ENCYCLOPEDIA	PERIODICAL DATABASE	INTERNET

Name: _____ Date: _____

Station One: *Locating Sources*

Directions: Locate the following types of sources in your school library to complete the chart.

Book	Encyclopedia
Access the card catalog and locate a book on earthquakes. Record the following information. Title: Author: Copyright date: Total number of pages:	Use a print or online encyclopedia to find an article about earthquakes. Answer the following questions. How long is the article? When was it copyrighted? Are pictures, maps, or tables included?
Periodical Database	**Internet**
Use a periodical database to locate an article about earthquakes. Record the following information. Title of article: Author: Title of magazine: Date of periodical: Page numbers:	Search for a website about earthquakes. Record the following information. URL: Title of website: Website owner: Date created or updated:

Student Instructions—Station Two: *Keyword Search*

Introduction

Read the following information. Use what you learn to complete the right-hand interactive notebook page.

Search strategies can be used to help improve online research. One strategy is the use of keywords. Keywords allow you to search specific words or phrases related to your topic. Another strategy is combining keywords and search operators to limit or expand your search results to locate the most relevant information on your topic.

Search Operators		
Operators	**Meaning**	**Strategy**
+	The **+** symbol means the same as the word **AND**. **Example:** cow +Angus	To limit search results
-	The **-** symbol means the same as the word **NOT**. **Example:** cow -Hereford	To exclude specific words
OR	The word **OR** means to search for either word. **Example:** cow OR Angus	To expand search results
" "	Quotation marks mean search for that specific phrase. **Example:** "certified Angus beef"	To limit the search to a specific phrase

How to Create Your Right-hand Interactive Notebook Page

Complete the following steps on a blank page on the right-hand side of a notebook. If you already have an interactive notebook, complete these steps on a blank page on the right-hand side of your current interactive notebook.

Step 1: Cut out the title and glue it to the top of the notebook page.

Step 2: Cut out the description pieces and glue in the correct box on the chart.

Step 3: Complete the chart by giving an example for each operator.

Step 4: Cut out the "Search Operators" chart and glue it under the title on the notebook page.

Demonstrate and Reflect on What You Have Learned

At the learning station, use this page and the right-hand interactive notebook page you created to help you complete the activity.

Keyword Search

Search Operators		
Operators	Meaning	Give an Example
+		
-		
OR		
" "		

The + symbol means the same as the word **AND**.	The - symbol means the same as the word **NOT**.
The word **OR** means to search for either word.	Quotation marks mean search for that specific phrase.

Name: _____   Date: _____

Station Two: *Keyword Search*

Directions: Your research topic is **Adoption of Wild Mustangs**. Go online and search the five keywords or phrases listed below. Record the number of search results you receive for each word.

Topic: Adoption of Wild Mustangs

Keyword: *horse*   Number of Search Results: _____

Keyword: *horses*   Number of Search Results: _____

Keyword: *mustang*   Number of Search Results: _____

Keyword: *mustangs*   Number of Search Results: _____

Phrase: *"wild mustangs"*   Number of Search Results: _____

Limit or Expand an Internet Search

Directions: Go online. Type each search term and record the number of search results you receive for each combination.

Mustang OR Mustangs   Number of Search Results: _____

Mustang +adoption   Number of Search Results: _____

Mustang -car   Number of Search Results: _____

"adoption of wild mustangs"   Number of Search Results: _____

Reflection: What effect did the use of operators have on your Internet search? Write your response on the lines below. Be prepared to share your experience during class discussion.

_____

_____

_____

_____

Student Instructions—Station Three: *Evaluating Internet Sources*

Introduction

Read the following information. Use what you learn to complete the right-hand interactive notebook page.

There is a lot of information on the Internet, but not all of it is factual or reliable. Before using information from an Internet source, be sure to follow three basics steps.

1. Determine if the information is useful.
2. Compare the information to information in other sources (databases, encyclopedias, books, magazines, newspapers).
3. Use the following criteria to help you evaluate each source.
    Author/Creator
    *   *Who created this information?*
    *   *What are the author's credentials (education, knowledge, experience, occupation)?*

    Point of View/Bias
    *   *What is the person's point of view or perspective?*
    *   *Is the information objective, or can you detect bias?*

    Audience/Purpose
    *   *Who is the intended audience?*
    *   *Why was the information created (to inform, persuade, entertain, or describe)?*

    Content/Reliability
    *   *Is the information up to date?*
    *   *Are the links up to date and working?*
    *   *What organization or institution is associated with or sponsored the site: government (.gov), school (.edu), military (.mil), organization (.org), or company or business (.com)?*

How to Create Your Right-hand Interactive Notebook Page

Complete the following steps on a blank page on the right-hand side of a notebook. If you already have an interactive notebook, complete these steps on a blank page on the right-hand side of your current interactive notebook.

Step 1: Cut out the title and glue it to the top of the notebook page.
Step 2: Cut out the four flaps. Apply glue to the back of the top sections and attach each to the page.
Step 3: Cut out the question strips and glue them under the appropriate flaps.

Demonstrate and Reflect on What You Have Learned

At the learning station, use this page and the right-hand interactive notebook page you created to help you complete the activity. Then write a reflection statement in your notebook about the importance of evaluating Internet sources when doing research.

Evaluating Internet Sources

Author/Creator

Point of View/Bias

Audience/Purpose

Content/Reliability

Is the information up to date? Are the links up to date and working? What organization or institution is associated with or sponsored the site?
Who is the intended audience? Why was the information created?
What is the author's point of view or perspective? Is the information objective, or can you detect bias?
Who created this information? What are the author's credentials?

Name: _____ Date: _____

Station Three: *Evaluating Internet Sources*

Directions: Go online and access one of the websites on the "Battle of Gettysburg Websites" handout. Use information from the website to complete the chart.

Website Evaluation	
Website URL:	
Title of the website:	
Question	**Answer**
Who owns the website (individual, business, institution, government, organization, etc.)?	Answer:
What are the credentials of the author/publisher of the website?	Answer:
What is the purpose of the website?	Answer:
Who is the intended audience?	Answer:
Does the information contain bias?	Answer:
When was the information last updated?	Answer:
Are the links up to date and working?	Answer:
What organization or institution is associated with or sponsored the site?	Answer:

Handout—Station Three: *Battle of Gettysburg Websites*

American Civil War—The Battle of Gettysburg
<http://www.ducksters.com/history/battle_of_gettysburg.php>

Battle of Gettysburg
<http://www.history.com/topics/american-civil-war/battle-of-gettysburg>

Battle of Gettysburg: American Civil War [1863]
<http://www.britannica.com/event/Battle-of-Gettysburg>

Battle of Gettysburg, 1863
<http://www.eyewitnesstohistory.com/gtburg.htm>

Battle of Gettysburg: Prelude to Battle
<http://www.militaryhistoryonline.com/gettysburg/>

Gettysburg
<http://www.civilwar.org/battlefields/gettysburg.html>

Gettysburg Foundation—Battle of Gettysburg
<http://www.gettysburgfoundation.org/37>

Gettysburg: National Military Park, Pennsylvania
<https://www.nps.gov/gett/index.htm>

Great Battle of Gettysburg, The
<http://www.nationalreview.com/article/352377/great-battle-gettysburg-mackubin-thomas-owens>

Turning Point of the Civil War…Gettysburg
<https://www.loc.gov/wiseguide/july03/civil.html>

Student Instructions—Station Four: *Creating a Bibliography*

What You Need to Know

Read the following information. Use what you learn to complete the right-hand interactive note-book page.

As you research, you will take notes from many different types of sources, such as books, encyclopedias, magazine articles, interviews, and websites. It is important to keep track of your research trail. After your research is completed, you will create a bibliographic citation for each source. There are different styles to use when writing citations. Your teacher or school librarian will tell you which one is preferred. The citations are then compiled to create a bibliography. A bibliography is an alphabetical list of all the print and nonprint sources from which you used in-formation. Your teacher may ask you to turn in a bibliography before making your presentation.

How to Create Your Right-hand Interactive Notebook

Complete the following steps on a blank page on the right-hand side of a notebook. If you already have an interactive notebook, complete these steps on a blank page on the right-hand side of your current interactive notebook.

Step 1: Cut out the title and glue it to the top of the notebook page.
Step 2: Cut out the definition for a bibliography and glue it under the title.
Step 3: Cut out the five word pieces and the five bibliographic citation format strips.
Step 4: Glue the word piece labeled "Book" under the definition. Under the word "Book" glue its corresponding citation strip.
Step 5: Repeat for each word piece and citation strip in the following order: Encyclopedia, Journal, Magazine, and Website.

Demonstrate and Reflect on What You Have Learned

At the learning station, use this page, the right-hand interactive notebook page you created, and the "How to Format a Bibliography" handout to help you complete the activity. After completing the activity, arrange the four bibliographic citations into a bibliography. Copy the bibliography on your left-hand interactive notebook page. Then write a reflection paragraph comparing the two methods for creating bibliographic citations.

Remember to:

- begin the first line of a citation at the left-hand margin. Each of the following lines for the citation is indented under the first line.

- sort the citations into alphabetical order by using the first word of each citation.

Creating a Bibliography

A **bibliography** is an alphabetical list of all the print and nonprint sources from which you used information.

Author's last name, Author's first name. <u>Title of Book</u>.
   Place of Publication: Publisher, Copyright Date.

Author's last name, Author's first name. "Title of Article."
   <u>Title of Encyclopedia</u>. Edition.

Author's last name, Author's first name. "Title of Article."
   <u>Title of Journal</u>. Volume. Issue (Date): Page Numbers.

Author's last name, Author's first name. "Title of Article."
   <u>Title of Magazine</u>. Publication Date: Page Numbers.

Author's last name, Author's first name. "Title of Article/Webpage."
   <u>Title of Website</u>. Date of Last Revision. Organization Title.
   Access Date. <Website URL>.

Book	Encyclopedia	Journal
Magazine	Website	

Name: _____   Date: _____

Station Four: *Creating a Bibliography*

Directions: At the learning station, you will find four sources. Select two of the sources and create a bibliographic citation for each. Write the citations in the appropriate boxes below. For the other two sources, go online and access a bibliographic citation maker website to create the citations. Copy these citations in the appropriate boxes below.

Source 1: Book

Source 2: Encyclopedia article

Source 3: Magazine article

Source 4: Website

Handout—Station Four: *How to Format a Bibliography*

Format for Bibliographic Citations

Book

Author	*Title of Book*	*Place of Publication*
Williams, Sarah M.	People in History.	Chicago:

Publisher	*Copyright Date*
Madison Publishing,	2014.

Encyclopedia

Author	*Title of Article*
Bishop, Kate.	"Abraham Lincoln."

Title of Encyclopedia	*Edition*
The World International Encyclopedia,	2015 ed.

Magazine

Author	*Title of Article*	*Title of Magazine*
Palmer, Paul.	"The Death of Lincoln Revisited."	Civil War Historical Review.

Publication Date	*Page Numbers*
Dec. 2015:	15–23.

Website

Author	*Title of Article/Webpage*	*Title of Website*	*Date of Last Revision*
Hudson, Jason.	"Abraham Lincoln."	U.S. Presidents.	27 January 2016.

Organization Title	*Access Date*	*Website URL*
Presidential Historical Association.	10 April 2016.	<http://www.preshistory.org>.

Sample Bibliography

Bishop, Kate. "Abraham Lincoln." The World International Encyclopedia, 2015 ed.

Hudson, Jason. "Abraham Lincoln." U.S. Presidents. 27 January 2016.
   Presidential Historical Association. 10 April 2016. <http://www.preshistory.org>.

Palmer, Paul. "The Death of Lincoln Revisited." Civil War Historical Review.
   Dec. 2015: 15–23.

Williams, Sarah M. People in History. Chicago: Madison Publishing, 2014.

Teacher Page

Unit: Opinions, Claims, and Evidence

Goal: Students will demonstrate an understanding of how to use evidence or details to support claims or opinions.

Common Core State Standards (CCSS):

6th Grade	7th Grade	8th Grade
SL.6.3 Delineate a speaker's argument and specific claims, distinguishing claims that are supported by reasons and evidence from claims that are not. SL.6.4 Present claims and findings, sequencing ideas logically and using pertinent descriptions, facts, and details to accentuate main ideas or themes; use appropriate eye contact, adequate volume, and clear pronunciation.	SL.7.3 Delineate a speaker's argument and specific claims, evaluating the soundness of the reasoning and the relevance and sufficiency of the evidence. SL.7.4 Present claims and findings, emphasizing salient points in a focused, coherent manner with pertinent descriptions, facts, details, and examples; use appropriate eye contact, adequate volume, and clear pronunciation.	SL.8.3 Delineate a speaker's argument and specific claims, evaluating the soundness of the reasoning and relevance and sufficiency of the evidence and identifying when irrelevant evidence is introduced. SL.8.4 Present claims and findings, emphasizing salient points in a focused, coherent manner with relevant evidence, sound, valid reasoning, and well-chosen details; use appropriate eye contact, adequate volume, and clear pronunciation.

© Copyright 2010. National Governors Association Center for Best Practices and Council of Chief State School Officers. All rights reserved.

Materials List/Setup

Station One: *Stating Your Opinion* (Activity)   Station Two: *Choosing Sides* (Activity)
Station Three: *Supporting Details* (Activity)
Station Four: *Using Relevant Evidence* (Activity); *Abraham Lincoln and Fifty Years of Freedom* (Handout)

Activity: one copy per student   Handout: one copy per each student in a group

Opening: Discussion Questions (Teacher-Directed)

1. What is a claim?
2. What is the difference between a fact and an opinion?

Student Instructions for Learning Stations

At the learning stations, you will explore forming an opinion, choosing sides, making claims, and providing evidence. Discuss your answers with other team members after completing each activity.

Closure: Reflection

The following questions can be used to stimulate discussion or as a journaling activity.
1. Why is it important to support claims with evidence?
2. Why is it important to research both sides of an argument?

Name: _____   Date: _____

Station One: *Stating Your Opinion*

Your opinion is your view or belief about something. Listed below are examples of beginning phrases often used when stating a personal opinion.

> *I believe that…*   *I think…*   *As for me…*
> *In my opinion…*   *I am convinced that…*   *In my experience…*
> *I feel that…*   *My personal view is…*   *As I see it…*

Directions: Complete the chart below. For each topic, state your opinion and the reason.

Topic	Opinion	Reason
Should classes be separated by gender?		
Should school lunches be free for everyone?		
Should students be allowed to use cell phones during class time?		
Should food and drink vending machines be banned from schools?		
Should middle-school students be allowed to go on overnight field trips?		

Name: _____ Date: _____

Station Two: *Choosing Sides*

Before entering into a discussion, it is important to know both sides of an issue, or the pros and cons. The **pros** are the advantages, and the **cons** are the disadvantages. Knowing both sides will help you formulate an opinion and can also be used to support your position during discussion.

Directions: Go online and research the discussion topic. Use your research to complete the chart. Then answer the questions.

> **Topic for Discussion**
>
> Middle-School Students Participating in Competitive Sports

What are the Pros? (Advantages)	What are the Cons? (Disadvantages)

What is your opinion about middle-school students participating in competitive sports?

What effect, if any, did your research have on your opinion?

Name: _____ Date: _____

Station Three: *Supporting Details*

Directions: Go online and research the discussion topic. Use your research to complete the chart.

Discussion Topic

Is breakfast the most important meal of the day?

⬇

State Your Opinion

⬇

Reason

⬇ ⬇ ⬇

Supporting Detail	**Supporting Detail**	**Supporting Detail**

Name: _____   Date: _____

Station Four: *Using Relevant Evidence*

To support a claim, a speaker must use evidence and sound reasoning. Some evidence is more relevant, or important, than others.

Directions: Read the "Abraham Lincoln and Fifty Years of Freedom" handout. During his speech, the speaker presents several pieces of evidence to support his view. Complete the graphic organizer by listing the four most relevant pieces of evidence.

Evidence #1

Evidence #2

Position of Dr. Alexander Walters:

President Abraham Lincoln was opposed to slavery.

Evidence #3

Evidence #4

Handout—Station Four:
Abraham Lincoln and Fifty Years of Freedom

The following is an excerpt from a speech entitled "Abraham Lincoln and Fifty Years of Freedom." It was presented by Dr. Alexander Walters, Bishop of A.M.E. Zion Church.

The assertion has been made that President Lincoln was not in favor of universal freedom. I beg to take issue with this view.

A careful study of this sincere, just, and sympathetic man will serve to show that from his earliest years he was against slavery. He declared again and again; "If slavery is not wrong, nothing is wrong; I cannot remember when I did not so think and feel."

Back in the thirties this young man clad in homespun was standing in the slave-mart of New Orleans, watching husbands and wives being separated forever, and children being doomed never again to look into the faces of their parents. As the hammer of the auctioneer fell, this young flat-boatman, with quivering lips, turned to his companion and said: "If ever I get a chance to hit that thing (slavery), I will hit it hard, by the Eternal God I will."

In March, 1839, he had placed upon the *House Journal of Illinois* a formal protest against pro-slavery resolutions which he could get but one other member beside himself to sign. Long before he was made President, in a speech at Charleston, Illinois, he said: "Yes we will speak for freedom, and against slavery, as long as the Constitution of our country guarantees free speech, until everywhere on this wide land the sun shall shine, and the rain shall fall, and the winds shall blow upon no man who goes forth to unrequited toil."

While in Congress in 1848 he offered a bill to abolish slavery in the District of Columbia. It was his opinion that Congress had control over the institution of slavery in the District of Columbia and the territories, and he evidenced his desire for the freedom of the slaves by offering a bill to abolish it in the District, and he afterwards strenuously advocated the elimination of slavery from the territories.

In 1864, about the time of the repeal of the Fugitive Slave Law, President Lincoln said to some gentlemen from the West: "There have been men base enough to propose to me to return to slavery our black warriors of Port Hudson and Olustee, and thus win the respect of the masters they fought. Should I do so, I should deserve to be damned in time and eternity."

Through all the mighty struggle of the Civil War when bowed in sorrow, and when it was truly said of him "That he was a man of sorrows and acquainted with grief," he was ever heard to say, "It is my desire that all men be free."

If President Lincoln were not in favor of the freedom of the slaves, why did he write the Emancipation Proclamation without the knowledge of his Cabinet and, when reading it to them, informed them that he did not do so to have them make any changes, but simply to apprise them

Handout—Station Four:
Abraham Lincoln and Fifty Years of Freedom (cont.)

of its contents? I answer, because he saw the time had come, the opportune time for which he had longed, when he, as President of these United States, could free the slaves. The South was so certain that it was Mr. Lincoln's intention to liberate the slaves, that upon his election as President, they seceded from the Union. They felt that the institution which they had struggled so long to maintain was doomed.

His famous letter to Horace Greeley, so diplomatically written, shows him to be in favor of the emancipation of slaves. Said he; "My paramount object is to save the Union, and not either to save or destroy slavery. If I could save the Union without freeing any slaves I would do it; if I could save it by freeing all the slaves I would do it; and if I could do it by freeing some and leaving others alone, I would also do that. I shall try to correct errors when shown to be errors, and I shall adopt new views as fast as they shall appear to be true views. I have here stated my purpose according to my views of official duty, and I intend no modification of my oft-expressed personal wish that all men everywhere could be free."

Had President Lincoln not desired the freedom of the slaves would he have written this last sentence?

(Excerpt from "Abraham Lincoln and Fifty Years of Freedom," by Alexander Walter, D.D. *Masterpieces of Negro Eloquence.* Edited by Alice Moore Dunbar, 1914)

Teacher Page

Unit: Multimedia Components and Visual Displays

Goal: Students will demonstrate an understanding of the importance of including multimedia components and visual displays in presentations.

Common Core State Standards (CCSS):

6th Grade	7th Grade	8th Grade
SL.6.2 Interpret information presented in diverse media and formats (e.g., visually, quantitatively, orally) and explain how it contributes to a topic, text, or issue under study. SL.6.5 Include multimedia components (e.g., graphics, images, music, sound) and visual displays in presentations to clarify information.	SL.7.2 Analyze the main ideas and supporting details presented in diverse media and formats (e.g., visually, quantitatively, orally) and explain how the ideas clarify a topic, text, or issue under study. SL.7.5 Include multimedia components and visual displays in presentations to clarify claims and findings and emphasize salient points.	SL.8.2 Analyze the purpose of information presented in diverse media and formats (e.g., visually, quantitatively, orally) and evaluate the motives (e.g., social, commercial, political) behind its presentation. SL.8.5 Integrate multimedia and visual displays into presentations to clarify information, strengthen claims and evidence, and add interest.

© Copyright 2010. National Governors Association Center for Best Practices and Council of Chief State School Officers. All rights reserved.

Materials List/Setup

Station One: *Creating a Visual Display* (Activity); *Roosevelt's First Fireside Chat* (Handout)
Station Two: *Visual Displays and Digital Media*
Station Three: *Creating an Emotional Impact*
Station Four: *Designing a Multimedia Presentation*

Activity: one copy per student
Handout: one copy per each student in a group

Opening: Discussion Questions (Teacher-Directed)

1. What is a multimedia presentation?
2. What are some types of visual displays used in presentations?

Student Instructions for Learning Stations

At the learning stations, you will explore the contribution of multimedia components to presentations. Discuss your answers with other team members after completing each activity.

Closure: Reflection

The following questions can be used to stimulate discussion or as a journaling activity.
1. What are some components of an effective multimedia presentation?
2. How do visual displays help the audience better understand the presentation?

Station One: *Creating a Visual Display*

Web Address: <http://www.americanrhetoric.com/speeches/fdrfirstfiresidechat.html>
Title: Franklin Delano Roosevelt, First Fireside Chat, "The Banking Crisis"
Source: AmericanRhetoric.com

Directions: Read "Roosevelt's First Fireside Chat" handout. Next, go online to the above web address. Listen to the portion of President Roosevelt's speech included on the handout. Focus on the third paragraph of his radio address. On a separate sheet of paper, use the graphics below to create a visual display that best illustrates what President Roosevelt is describing in this paragraph.

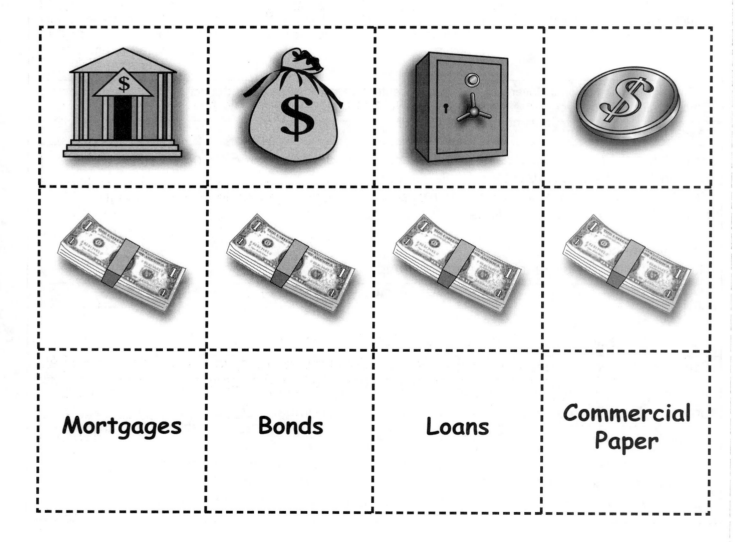

| Mortgages | Bonds | Loans | Commercial Paper |

Name: _____ Date: _____

Station Two: *Visual Displays and Digital Media*

Web Address: <https://www.ted.com/talks/jedidah_isler_how_i_fell_in_love_with_quasars_blazars_and_our_incredible_universe>
Title: "Jedidah Isler: How I fell in love with quasars, blazars and our incredible universe."
Source: TED2015. Filmed Mar 2015. (04:19). [Interactive transcript is provided.]

Directions: Go online to the above web address. Listen to the presentation, and record your observations on the chart below. Use your observations to answer the reflection question.

What I Observed	
Visual Display	What type of graphic elements (graphs, diagrams, tables, etc.) did the presenter include in her presentation?
Digital Media	What type of digital media (images, video, audio, etc.) did the presenter include in her presentation?
Audience Reaction	What evidence did you observe concerning the audience's reaction to the presentation?

Reflection: Did the use of visual displays and digital media clarify the information presented, or did it distract from the presentation? Use your observations to support your answer. Write the answer in the box below.

Name: _____   Date: _____

Station Three: *Creating an Emotional Impact*

> **Web Address:** <https://www.youtube.com/watch?v=EU-IBF8nwSY>
> **Title:** "Ronald Reagan TV Ad: It's Morning in America Again"
> **Length:** 01:00 minute

Directions: Go online to the above web address. View Ronald Reagan's 1984 presidential campaign advertisement. Use your observations to complete the chart. Then answer the questions below.

Text from the campaign ad	What images were used to represent the text?
"It's morning again in America"	
"Today more men and women will go to work than ever before in our country's history."	
"And, under the leadership of President Reagan, our country is prouder and stronger and better."	

1. What is the purpose of the voice-over narration?

2. How does the music add to the emotional impact of the advertisement?

Name: _____ Date: _____

Station Four: *Designing a Multimedia Presentation*

Directions: Read the prompt below. Then use a presentation program to design a multimedia presentation following the directions below.

> **Prompt:** You are the student-body president of Roosevelt Middle School. The school board is considering adopting a policy on requiring students to purchase and wear school uniforms. You have been asked to survey the students about the proposal and make a presentation at the next school-board meeting about your findings.

Survey Data

Survey Question: *Should the school board adopt a policy requiring students to purchase and wear school uniforms?*

Survey Results:

6th grade:	For:	Boys, 36	Girls, 27
	Against:	Boys, 25	Girls, 39
7th grade:	For:	Boys, 22	Girls, 18
	Against:	Boys, 43	Girls, 47
8th grade:	For:	Boys, 15	Girls, 16
	Against:	Boys, 49	Girls, 55

Directions: Use the following guidelines to design a five-slide presentation. Add appropriate color, font, and images.

Guidelines

Slide One	**Slide Two**	**Slide Three**
Title	Survey question	Graph displaying survey data
Your Name		
Date of Presentation		

Slide Four	**Slide Five**
Summary of the survey results	Leave this slide blank

Handout—Station One: *Roosevelt's First Fireside Chat*

On March 12, 1933, families gathered at home around the radio and listened to President Franklin D. Roosevelt deliver his first "fireside chat." The speech was given to inform listeners about his reasons for declaring a national banking holiday.

My friends:

I want to talk for a few minutes with the people of the United States about banking, to talk with the comparatively few who understand the mechanics of banking, but more particularly with the overwhelming majority of you who use banks for the making of deposits and the drawing of checks.

I want to tell you what has been done in the last few days, and why it was done, and what the next steps are going to be. I recognize that the many proclamations from State capitols and from Washington, the legislation, the Treasury regulations, and so forth, couched for the most part in banking and legal terms, ought to be explained for the benefit of the average citizen. I owe this, in particular, because of the fortitude and the good temper with which everybody has accepted the inconvenience and hardships of the banking holiday. And I know that when you understand what we in Washington have been about, I shall continue to have your cooperation as fully as I have had your sympathy and your help during the past week.

First of all, let me state the simple fact that when you deposit money in a bank, the bank does not put the money into a safe deposit vault. It invests your money in many different forms of credit: in bonds, in commercial paper, in mortgages and in many other kinds of loans. In other words, the bank puts your money to work to keep the wheels of industry and of agriculture turning around. A comparatively small part of the money that you put into the bank is kept in currency, an amount which in normal times is wholly sufficient to cover the cash needs of the average citizen. In other words, the total amount of all the currency in the country is only a comparatively small proportion of the total deposits in all the banks of the country.

(Transcript: Excerpt from Franklin Delano Roosevelt, Fireside Chat "The Banking Crisis")

Teacher Page

Unit: Verbal and Nonverbal Communication

Goal: Students will demonstrate an understanding of verbal and nonverbal communication skills.

Common Core State Standards (CCSS):

6th Grade	7th Grade	8th Grade
SL 6.4 Present claims and findings, sequencing ideas logically and using pertinent descriptions, facts, and details to accentuate main ideas or themes; use appropriate eye contact, adequate volume, and clear pronunciation.	SL 7.4 Present claims and findings, emphasizing salient points in a focused, coherent manner with pertinent descriptions, facts, details, and examples; use appropriate eye contact, adequate volume, and clear pronunciation.	SL 8.4 Present claims and findings, emphasizing salient points in a focused, coherent manner with relevant evidence, sound valid reasoning, and well-chosen details; use appropriate eye contact, adequate volume, and clear pronunciation.

© Copyright 2010. National Governors Association Center for Best Practices and Council of Chief State School Officers. All rights reserved.

Materials List/Setup

Station One: *Delivering a Speech* (Activity)
Station Two: *Practicing Verbal Techniques* (Activity)
Station Three: *Detecting Verbal Communication* (Activity)
Station Four: *Observing Nonverbal Communication* (Activity)

Activity: one copy per student
Handout: one copy of "Verbal and Nonverbal Delivery Techniques" posted at each learning station.

Opening: Discussion Questions (Teacher-Directed)

1. What is the difference between verbal and nonverbal communication?
2. What are some techniques speakers use when making a presentation?

Student Instructions for Learning Stations

At the learning stations, you will explore techniques used by effective public speakers. Discuss your answers with other team members after completing each activity.

Closure: Reflection

The following questions can be used to stimulate discussion or as a journaling activity.
1. What are some tips for becoming an effective public speaker?
2. Why is it important to pay close attention to the verbal and nonverbal signals of a speaker?

Name: _____ Date: _____

Station One: *Delivering a Speech*

We express a great deal of meaning by the way we use our voices. Pausing briefly after a punctuation mark, emphasizing important words, increasing or decreasing the volume, and changing the pitch of your voice help listeners to better understand the presentation.

Directions: Below is the text of Lincoln's "Gettysburg Address." Read the text aloud. Make the following notations on the speech. Once more read the address aloud, using the notations to help improve your delivery. Practice the delivery multiple times before presenting your interpretation to team members or the class.

Notations to Mark

- Punctuation: Punctuation marks are a good time to briefly pause in order to take a breath or emphasize certain words. Underline each punctuation mark.
- Words: Some words in a sentence are more important than others. These words are known as keywords, and they receive more emphasis through pausing and changes to pitch and volume. Circle all keywords.
- Volume and Pitch: Vary the volume and pitch of your voice to hold the audience's attention. Use an arrow pointing up when you want to increase the volume or raise the pitch of your voice. Use an arrow pointing down when you want to decrease the volume or lower the pitch of your voice.

On November 19, 1863, President Abraham Lincoln delivered his now famous speech at the dedication ceremony of the Gettysburg Memorial Cemetery.

The Gettysburg Address [Transcription]

Four score and seven years ago our fathers brought forth, upon this continent, a new nation, conceived in Liberty, and dedicated to the proposition that all men are created equal.

Now we are engaged in a great civil war, testing whether that nation, or any nation so conceived, and so dedicated, can long endure. We are met on a great battlefield of that war. We have come to dedicate a portion of that field, as a final resting place for those who here gave their lives, that that nation might live. It is altogether fitting and proper that we should do this.

But, in a larger sense, we cannot dedicate—we cannot consecrate—we cannot hallow this ground. The brave men, living and dead, who struggled here, have consecrated it, far above our poor power to add or detract. The world will little note, nor long remember what we say here, but it can never forget what they did here. It is for us, the living, rather, to be dedicated here to the unfinished work which they who fought here have thus far so nobly advanced. It is rather for us to be here dedicated to the great task remaining before us—that from these honored dead we take increased devotion to that cause for which they have gave the last full measure of devotion—that we here highly resolve that these dead shall not have died in vain; that this nation, under God, shall have a new birth of freedom, and that government of the people, by the people, for the people, shall not perish from the earth.

Name: _____   Date: _____

Station Two: *Practicing Verbal Techniques*

A speaker should use a variety of verbal techniques. Volume and pitch can affect the tone of the message. Pace and rhythm can be used to emphasize words or hold the attention of the audience.

Directions: Complete the two activities below to practice verbal techniques.

Activity #1

Choose one of the sentences below and read it aloud multiple times. Each time, vary the volume or pitch in order to emphasize different words in the sentence and change the tone of the message. Next, practice varying the volume and pitch using each of the other sentences.

I didn't know she was the one who ate the cake.

Caleb went to the mall, but I stayed home.

Susan stole the ball and made a basket.

Who is running for student body president?

Everyone is invited to the party.

Activity #2

While varying the pace and rhythm, practice saying the following tongue twister clearly.

Betty Botta bought some butter;
"But," said she, "this butter's bitter!
If I put it in my batter
It will make my batter bitter.
But a bit o' better butter
Will but make my batter better."

Then she bought a bit o' butter
Better than the bitter butter,
Made her bitter batter better.
So 'twas better Betty Botta
Bought a bit o' better butter.

Name: _____ Date: _____

Station Three: *Detecting Verbal Communication*

> **Web Address:** <https://www.youtube.com/watch?v=g25G1M4EXrQ>
> **Title:** We Choose to Go to the Moon (9/12/62) [Clip] – John F. Kennedy Speech to Rice University (0.2:11)
> **Description:** President John F. Kennedy spoke at Rice University on the goals of the United States in the race to outer space.

Directions: Go online to the above web address and view the video clip. Use your observations to complete the chart. Then answer the question below.

Effective Use of Voice	
Verbal Signals	**Record Examples From the Speech**
Diction: The speaker pronounces words clearly so listeners can understand the presentation.	
Pitch: The speaker uses the rise and fall of his voice to affect the mood and tone of the message, which helps the audience remember the main points.	
Tempo: The speaker talks at a rate that allows listeners to follow and understand the topic. The speaker slows down or pauses to emphasize key points.	
Volume: The speaker presents speech at a level that allows everyone to hear clearly and increases or lowers volume to emphasize key points.	

Did the speaker effectively use his voice to deliver the speech? Use examples from the chart to support your answer. Write your answer in the box below.

Name: _____ Date: _____

Station Four: *Observing Nonverbal Communication*

Web Address: <https://www.ted.com/talks/david_pogue_10_top_time_saving_tech_tips?language=en>
Title: David Pogue: 10 Top Time-saving Tech Tips [Filmed Feb 2013 (05:44)]
Source: TED2013. Filmed Feb 2013. (05:44). [Interactive transcript is provided.]

Directions: Go online to the above web address and view the presentation. Use your observations to complete the chart. Then answer the question below.

Nonverbal Signals	Record Observations
Eye Contact Speaker maintains eye contact with the audience.	
Facial Expressions Speaker uses facial expressions such as smiling, frowning, or the raising of eyebrows.	
Body Movement Speaker uses gestures such as hand movements, shrugging, nodding, and shaking of head.	
Posture Speaker stands or sits tall and straight.	

How did the speaker's use of nonverbal communication enhance or distract from the message of the presentation? Use observations from the chart to support your answer. Write your answer in the box below.

Handout: *Verbal and Nonverbal Delivery Techniques*

When speaking to a group, it is important to connect with your audience. Body movements and voice can be used to enhance the understanding of your message and to engage the audience.

Directions: Review the verbal and nonverbal delivery techniques below.

Verbal Delivery	Nonverbal Delivery
Diction: Speak clearly, pronouncing the words correctly. Make sure to use the final sounds of words ("d", "t", and "ing").	**Body Language:** Avoid fidgeting, swaying, or rocking back and forth. Body movements and stance communicate a message to your audience.
Tone: Use a sincere tone that lets the audience know you're interested in the topic.	**Eye Contact:** Use eye contact to connect with your audience. This creates a link between the audience and presenter. Find several friendly faces in the crowd, and speak directly to them. Vary your eye contact between them.
Volume: Project your voice loudly and clearly. A speech cannot be successful if the audience cannot hear the speaker or cannot understand the words. Vary the volume of your tone to emphasize key points.	**Facial Expressions:** Use facial expressions such as smiling, frowning, and arched eyebrows to reflect your emotions concerning the topic.
Expression: Use as much vocal range as possible. Vocal range includes using a variety of pitches. Inflection is another part of expression. We often use a rising inflection at the end of a question. Vary your vocal expression to keep your voice from becoming monotonous.	**Gestures:** Hand and arm gestures should appear natural. They should be used to emphasize important points of your message. Avoid using overly dramatic gestures.
Rate: Adjust the rate of your speech to allow the audience to follow and understand the topic. Use pauses to highlight key points.	**Posture:** Maintain good posture. Stand tall with shoulders back and head held up.

Teacher Page

Unit: Collegial Discussions

Goal: Students will demonstrate an understanding of the role of an effective listener and contributor during one-on-one, small-group, and classroom discussions.

Common Core State Standards (CCSS):

6th Grade	7th Grade	8th Grade
SL.6.1.B Follow rules for collegial discussions, set specific goals and deadlines, and define individual roles as needed.	SL.7.1.B Follow rules for collegial discussions, track progress toward specific goals and deadlines, and define individual roles as needed.	SL.8.1.B Follow rules for collegial discussions and decision-making, track progress toward specific goals and deadlines, and define individual roles as needed.

© Copyright 2010. National Governors Association Center for Best Practices and Council of Chief State School Officers. All rights reserved.

Materials List/Setup

Station *One: Conducting Collegial Discussions* (Activity); *Guidelines for Collegial Discussions* (Handout)

Station Two: *Participating in Group Discussions* (Activity); *Guidelines for Collegial Discussions* (Handout)

Station Three: *Preparing for Both Sides of a Discussion* (Activity); *Guidelines for Collegial Discussions* (Handout)

Station Four: *The Importance of Listening* (Activity)

Station Five: *Applying Listening Skills* (Activity); *Effective Listening Skills* (Handout)

Activity: one copy per student
Handout: one copy per each student in a group

Opening: Discussion Questions (Teacher-Directed)

1. What expectations do you have for yourself and others during discussion time?
2. What is the difference between verbal and nonverbal communication?

Student Instructions for Learning Stations

At the learning stations, you will explore skills necessary to become an effective listener and contributor. Discuss your answers with other team members after completing each activity.

Closure: Reflection

The following questions can be used to stimulate discussion or as a journaling activity.
1. What are some important guidelines to follow in any type of discussion?
2. Why is it important to pay close attention to the verbal and nonverbal cues of a speaker?

Name: _____ Date: _____

Station One: *Conducting Collegial Discussions*

Collegial discussions are respectful conversations between students engaged in one-on-one, small-group, or classroom discussions.

Directions: Read the "Guidelines for Collegial Discussions" handout. Follow the steps below to prepare for and conduct a small-group discussion on each topic listed in the chart.

Step 1: As a group, choose the team captain. The captain assigns the discussion roles.
Step 2: Prepare for discussion by listing what you already know about each topic on the chart below. Set a time limit.
Step 3: Conduct the discussion using collegial discussion guidelines.
Step 4: The group reporter shares a summary of the discussion with the class.

Topic	My Opinion
Should pennies be eliminated as part of the United States money system?	Agree or Disagree: My reasons:
Should school officials be allowed to search student lockers or backpacks without the student's permission?	Agree or Disagree: My reasons:

Name: _____ Date: _____

Station Two: *Participating in Group Discussions*

Directions: Read the "Guidelines for Collegial Discussions" handout. Follow the steps below to prepare for and conduct a small-group discussion on the topic listed in the chart.

Step 1: As a group, choose the team captain. The captain assigns the discussion roles.
Step 2: Prepare for discussion by recording your ideas and opinions about the topic on the "Student Response" chart below. Set a time limit.
Step 3: Conduct the discussion using collegial discussion guidelines.
Step 4: The group reporter shares a summary of the discussion with the class.

Student Response

Which classes?	*Number of minutes per night?*
Should middle-school students be assigned homework?	
Weekends?	*Game nights?*

Name: _____ Date: _____

Station Three: *Preparing for Both Sides of a Discussion*

Directions: Read the "Guidelines for Collegial Discussions" handout. Follow the steps below to prepare for and conduct a small-group discussion on the topic listed in the chart.

Step 1: As a group, choose the team captain. The captain assigns the discussion roles.
Step 2: Prepare for discussion by recording your ideas and opinions about the topic on the "Student Response" chart below. Set a time limit.
Step 3: Conduct the discussion using collegial discussion guidelines.
Step 4: The group reporter shares a summary of the discussion with the class.

Student Response

Advantages	*Disadvantages*

Should students attend year-round school?

Your Opinion

Reflection: What effect, if any, did the discussion have on your opinion of year-round school?

_____

_____

_____

_____

Name: _____ Date: _____

Station Four: *The Importance of Listening*

Directions: Complete the chart. Then answer the reflection question.

Person	Why is it important for this person to have good listening skills?
Television reporter	
Doctor	
Police Officer	
Student	
Sports Team Member	
Juror	
Parents	
Waiter	
Soldier	
Volunteer	
Construction Worker	

Reflection: What did you learn about the importance of listening?

_____

_____

Name: _____ Date: _____

Station Five: *Applying Listening Skills*

Directions: Follow the steps below to prepare for the listening activity. Then answer the questions to help determine if you were an effective listener.

Step 1: Read the "Guidelines for Collegial Discussions" and "Effective Listening Skills" handouts.

Step 2: As a group, choose the team captain. The captain assigns the discussion roles.

Step 3: Prepare for discussion by listing your favorite titles and genres of movies on a separate piece of paper. (Time limit: 5 minutes).

Step 4: Conduct a discussion on the topic of "my favorite movies" using collegial discussion guidelines.

Step 5: Use what you heard during discussion to answer the questions below.

Questions:

1. What movies were named most frequently? _____

   _____

   _____

2. What was the most popular movie genre? _____

3. Did members of your group: **[Circle: Yes or No]**

   • discuss the topic courteously?   Yes   No

   • take turns talking?   Yes   No

   • stray from the topic being discussed?   Yes   No

   • encourage others to take part in the discussion?   Yes   No

   • pay attention to each speaker?   Yes   No

   • acknowledge that other students made good points?   Yes   No

   • remain respectful when disagreeing with a speaker?   Yes   No

Reflection: What did you learn from this activity that will make you a better listener?

_____

_____

_____

_____

Handout: *Guidelines for Collegial Discussions*

An effective group discussion ensures that all members of the group come prepared to exchange their ideas and express their opinions. During discussion, each person will have the opportunity to speak freely while also respectfully listening to the views of others.

Discussion Roles and Responsibilities
The **Team Captain** assigns the roles listed below, announces the topic or question to be discussed, starts the discussion and keeps it moving, and returns the group to the topic when discussion strays.
The **Recorder** takes notes on important thoughts expressed by group members and writes a summary of the group discussion.
The **Reporter** shares a summary of the group discussion with the entire class.
The **Materials Manager** distributes and collects handouts.
The **Timekeeper** keeps track of time limits.
The **Monitor** reminds everyone of noise level and necessity of being respectful during discussion.

Guidelines for Discussion
Respectfully share your ideas and knowledge.
Be sure to stay on topic.
Wait until it is your turn to speak before sharing your ideas or asking questions.
If you do not understand a point being made by a member of the group, ask them to explain it more clearly.

Sentence Starters for Discussion
Agreement: I agree with _____ (speaker's name) because _____. I share _____ (speaker's name) view on _____.
Disagreement: I disagree with _____ (speaker's name) because _____. I do not share _____ (speaker's name) view on _____.
Clarification: What did you mean when you said _____? Can you give an example to explain _____?
Confusion: I am confused about _____. I do not understand what you meant when you said _____.

Handout: *Effective Listening Skills*

Being a good listener is important and necessary for your success as a student. The strategies below will help you become a better listener.

Courteous Listeners...

- Show they are ready to listen by sitting up straight and facing the speaker.

- Sit quietly without causing distractions.

- Stay focused on the speaker and the message.

- Use nonverbal communication, such as nodding of the head, smiling, or eye contact, to show interest or support.

- Pay attention, even if they disagree with the speaker.

- Wait until the end of the speech to respectfully ask questions or make comments.

Good Listeners...

- Focus on the message instead of the speaker's appearance.

- Ignore distractions.

- Identify the purpose of the presentation (to persuade, inform, or entertain).

- Listen for the main ideas and supporting details.

- Determine if the speaker is presenting facts, opinions, or both.

- Connect new information to prior knowledge or personal experiences.

- Visualize what they are hearing to increase understanding.

- Take notes in order to remember important points.

- Offer feedback and ask questions.

Answer Keys

*If applicable, answers were provided.

Unit: Research (Interactive Notebook)
Station One: Locating Sources (pg. 6)
(Answers will vary depending on the sources selected by the students.)

Station Two: Key Word Search (pg. 9)
(Answers will require teacher verification.)

Station Three: Evaluating Internet Sources (pg. 12)
(Answers will vary depending on the website selected by the students.)

Station Four: Creating a Bibliography (pg. 16)
(Answers will vary depending on the sources the teacher decides to use with the activity.)

Unit: Opinions, Claims, and Evidence
Station One: Stating Your Opinion (pg. 19)
(Answers will require teacher verification.)

Station Two: Choosing Sides (pg. 20)
(Answers will vary, but may include.)
Pros: teaches sportsmanship; provides socialization; promotes physical exercise; builds character; builds teamwork skills
Cons: physical injuries; loss of free time; pressure to perform; games are often held on school nights; expensive to travel to away games

Station Three: Supporting Details (pg. 21)
(Answers will require teacher verification.)

Station Four: Using Relevant Evidence (pg. 22)
• In March 1839, Lincoln "placed upon the *House Journal of Illinois* a formal protest against pro-slavery resolutions."
• In 1848, Lincoln "offered a bill to abolish slavery in the District of Columbia."
• Lincoln wrote the Emancipation Proclamation "without the knowledge of his Cabinet and, when reading it to them, informed them that he did not do so to have them make any changes, but simply to apprise them of its contents."

• In a letter to Horace Greeley he wrote, "I intend no modification of my oft-expressed personal wish that all men everywhere could be free."
(Other examples from the handout may be used.)

Unit: Multimedia Components and Visual Displays
Station One: Creating a Visual Display (pg. 26)
(Answers will require teacher verification.)

Station Two: Visual Displays and Digital Media (pg. 27)
Visual Display: diagram
Digital Media: images, artist drawing
Audience Reaction: The audience was focused on the speaker; sitting quietly; not talking among themselves; and applauded the speaker at the end of the talk.

Station Three: Creating an Emotional Impact (pg. 28)
(Answers will vary, but may include.)
It's morning again in America
Images: city skyline; boat in a harbor; lights on in buildings
Today more men and women…
Images: farmer on a tractor; boy throwing newspapers; people walking; people carrying briefcases; and man leaving his house getting into a car
And, under the leadership of President…
Images: flag flying: raising of a flag by a veteran
1. It sets a calming tone for the advertisement.
2. It promotes a positive perception of President Reagan.

Station Four: Designing a Multimedia Presentation (pg. 29)
(Answers will require teacher verification.)

Unit: Verbal and Nonverbal Communication
Station Three: Detecting Verbal Communication (pg. 34)
(Answers will vary, but may include.)
Diction: Kennedy emphasizes the ending sounds of words, especially words ending in "d" or "ed." Ex.: determined, deterred, and beyond
Pitch:
Rise: The following words or phrases are examples of when Kennedy's voice rises in pitch. Ex.: "all"; "Man in his quest for knowledge and progress is determined and cannot be deterred. The exploration of space will go ahead whether we join in it or not"; "to solve them for the good of all men"; and "We choose to go to the moon. We choose to go the moon. We choose to go the moon in this decade and do the other things and beyond not because it is easy, but because they are hard."
Fall: The following words or phrases are examples of when Kennedy's voice falls in pitch. Ex.: "overcome"; "our hopes for peace and security"; and "one we intend to win."
Tempo: Kennedy pauses for emphasis on key points. In the first sentence he pauses on the words: Bradford; 1630; Colony; actions; accompanied; difficulties.
Volume: He raises the volume with the rise of pitch and lowers the volume with the fall of pitch. See examples above under pitch.
Question: (Response will require teacher verification.)

Station Four: Observing Nonverbal Communication
(pg. 35)
(Answers will vary, but may include.)
Eye Contact: continually looks at audience
Facial Expressions: smiles, raises eyebrows
Body Movements: points at audience; lots of hand and arm gestures; points to slide presentation and to himself; waves bye to audience as leaving stage

Posture: He is relaxed as he walks around stage while giving presentation.
Question: (Response will require teacher verification.)

Unit: Collegial Discussions
Station One: Conducting Collegial Discussions (pg. 38)
(Answers will require teacher verification.)

Station Two: Participating in Group Discussions (pg. 39)
(Answers will require teacher verification.)

Station Three: Preparing for Both Sides of a Discussion (pg. 40)
(Answers will vary, but may include.)
Advantages: students engaged in learning for the majority of the year; allows students to re-energize and recharge over short breaks; school facilities used all year instead of sitting empty during summer break; reduces student absences and burnout with more extended time off throughout the year; students less likely to forget material over a short break than over a long summer vacation
Disadvantages: students might feel overwhelmed with the seemingly endless cycle of year-round school; some students might find it difficult to refocus after a short break; students benefitting from summer school might miss out on remedial or supplemental classes; students would not be able to take extended vacations with family; students may not be able to attend summer camps

Station Four: The Importance of Listening (pg. 41)
(Answers will require teacher verification.)

Station Five: Applying Listening Skills (pg. 42)
(Answers will require teacher verification.)